THE BIG ISLAND

THE BIG ISLAND

A Story of Isle Royale

Julian May ILLUSTRATIONS BY John Schoenherr

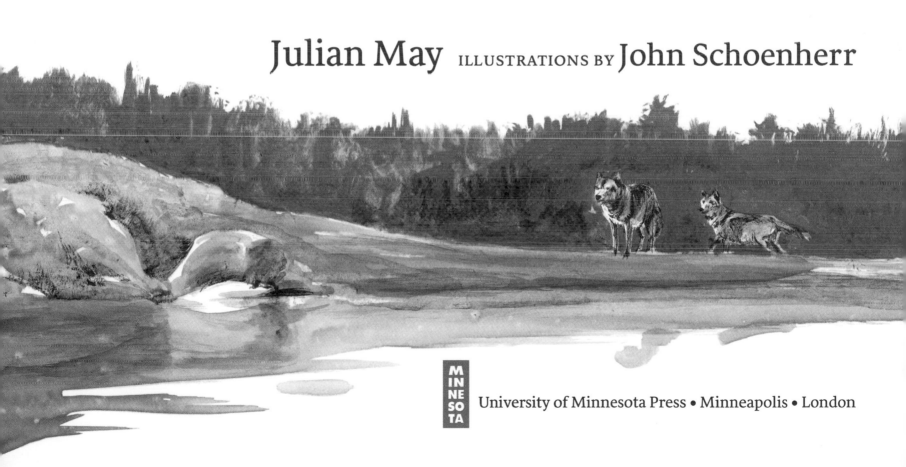

University of Minnesota Press • Minneapolis • London

AUTHOR'S NOTE FROM ORIGINAL PUBLICATION
This is a simplified version of an ecological situation that came to exist on Isle Royale in Lake Superior. The area is now a wilderness national park accessible by boat or plane. I would like to express my gratitude to Dr. L. David Mech, Museum of Natural History, University of Minnesota, for reading the manuscript of this book and making many helpful comments and suggestions.

First published in 1968 by Follett Publishing Company

First University of Minnesota Press edition, 2021

Text copyright 1968 by Julian May

Illustrations copyright 1968 by John Schoenherr

Published by the University of Minnesota Press
111 Third Avenue South, Suite 290
Minneapolis, MN 55401-2520
http://www.upress.umn.edu

Art prepared for printing by color specialist Timothy Meegan.

ISBN 978-1-5179-1069-3 (hc)
A Cataloging-in-Publication record for this title is available from the Library of Congress.

Printed in China on acid-free paper

The University of Minnesota is an equal-opportunity educator and employer.

29 28 27 26 25 24 23 22 21   10 9 8 7 6 5 4 3 2 1

To the McCargo Cove voyageurs:
wild strawberries forever

Up north is a big, deep lake. It was made long ago when a sea of ice melted. As years went by, the lake grew a little smaller and not so deep. A big island showed its head as the waters went down. At first the big island had only rocks on it. But soon plant seeds came floating and blowing, and green things began to grow.

Animals came to the big island, too. They came even though the island was far out in the lake. The beavers swam there.

Some animals took a ride and found a new home. Some animals came in winter when there was ice on the lake.

Other animals never came to the big island at all.

They stayed on the other shore.

The animals on the island lived together. Some of them ate plant food. Other animals ate meat. There were never too many of any one kind of animal.

Many years went by. People came to the big island.

They called it Isle Royale.

One year there was a very cold winter. The animals on the island did not care about the cold. They had plenty of food.

Some moose lived on the shore across the lake. They were
hungry. It was too snowy for them to find food. One large
moose saw the island far, far away across the icy water.
Maybe there was food there. Moose are good swimmers.
The large moose went into the water and began swimming
toward the island.

Other moose followed him. They all swam fifteen miles across the cold, deep water. The moose saw food on the island. All of them began to eat. Later, when there was a lot of ice on the lake, more moose came to the island. They walked over the ice.

Spring came. Each mother moose had a baby. One mother had two! The babies ate plant food. There was plenty for all of them. The baby moose grew up. They became new mothers and fathers.

The meat-eaters on the island could kill and eat small
animals, but they could not kill the moose. Moose were
too big and strong. Many years passed and there came
to be hundreds and hundreds of moose on the big island.
No meat-eater could bother them.

More and more moose were born each year. Not all of them could find food. Many became sick. There were too many moose on the island. The big island became a park. The park rangers tried to feed the moose, but there were too many of them. The rangers took some moose away in boats.

More moose babies were born. Soon there were just as many moose as before. And all of them were hungry.

Across the lake, other moose lived on the shore. A wolf pack lived on the shore with the moose. The wolves ate only meat. They were big and strong and able to hunt the moose. The crowded moose on the big island were starving. But there were not too many moose on the shore, because the wolves fed on some of them.

One winter, a wolf pack hunted on the ice along the lake shore. Suddenly, the ice began to move. The ice became a boat and took the wolf pack across the lake to the big island. The wolves could not get back. They had a new home.

In spring, the people on the island found out about the
wolves. The wolves were feeding on moose meat. They ate
the very old moose and the sick moose. But they could not
harm healthy moose.

After a while, there were no longer too many moose on the big island. Those that were left shared the plant food. There was enough now for all of them to eat. You can go to the big island today and see many moose . . . and perhaps a wolf. The moose are healthy and strong. The wolves eat only those moose that are weak or sick. The wolves and the moose and other animals all live together. They all have plenty to eat.

IN 1968 I was fortunate to read the text of *The Big Island* before it was first published. A lot has changed on Isle Royale since then. I began studying wolves on the island in 1958, and I have seen many of these changes up close.

The greatest change came in recent years when the wolf population became too inbred. The population dropped further when a pair of wolves fell through the ice and drowned. Soon there were too few wolves to kill the many moose that lived on the island. The moose population was multiplying and eating too many plants. The island needed more wolves.

In 2018 and 2019 rangers from Isle Royale National Park brought nineteen wolves from the mainland to the big island. These new wolves had pups and killed some of the moose. Over time, after the wolves were brought to the island, there were again just the right number of wolves and moose living together on Isle Royale. Now the wolves, the moose, and the plants are healthier again, just as they are in *The Big Island*, a story that presents the basics of ecological balance in its depiction of this predator–prey relationship.

—L. David Mech, 2021

JULIAN MAY (1931–2017) was a popular writer of science fiction, fantasy, horror, and children's books. She is best remembered for her *Saga of Pliocene Exile* and *Galactic Milieu* series books. Between 1956 and 1981 she wrote more than 250 science and sports nonfiction books for children and young adults.

JOHN SCHOENHERR (1935–2010) was a prolific illustrator of science fiction and children's picture books. He won the 1988 Caldecott Medal for his illustrations to *Owl Moon* by Jane Yolen. He was posthumously inducted into the Science Fiction and Fantasy Hall of Fame in 2015.